Living Healthy
in an Unhealthy
World

NATURAL HEALING PUBLICATIONS

Published by Natural Healing Publications
P.O. Box 9459, Marina del Rey, California 90295
1-877-TEACH-ME (832-2463)

Library of Congress Catalog Card Number: PENDING
<u>Living Healthy in an Unhealthy World</u>

ISBN# 0-9671567-2-6

WARNING

This book is published under the First Amendment of the United States Constitution, which grants the right to discuss openly and freely all matters of public concern and to express viewpoints no matter how controversial or unaccepted they may be. However, Medical groups and Pharmaceutical companies have finally infiltrated and violated our sacred Constitution. Therefore we are forced to give you the following WARNINGS:

If you are ill or have been diagnosed with any disease, please consult a medical doctor before attempting any natural healing program.

Any one of the programs in this book could be potentially dangerous, even lethal, especially if you are seriously ill. Therefore, any natural method you learn about in this book may cause harm, instead of the benefit you seek.

ASK YOUR DOCTOR FIRST, but remember that the vast majority of doctors have no education in natural healing methods. They will probably discourage you from trying any of the programs in this book.

Appreciation

Thanks to Nellie J. McGary–my maternal grandmother– who provided me with sanctuary many, many, many times during my early explorations into the unknown.

Thanks Mom for teaching me how to think, not what to think. I love you for showing me how to live and how to die.

Love & Appreciation to Marga and Anand Alima for their perpetual support and participation in living life totally. We have experienced many adventures together, with more to come.

Special thanks to Dr. Richard Schulze, my soul brother and adventure comrade for more years than I can remember. He is a constant reflection of the flame of living life totally.

Many thanks to Anisha Jones for sharing with me her on-going commitment to creating her personal paradise and for bringing so much laughter into my life.

Thanks to Arthur Schulze for being a constant reminder of how much fun it is to play too hard and too long.

My deepest appreciation to all my teachers, especially to Dr. Randolph Stone and Osho.

Thanks to all my clients and students who have worked with me with such dedication, trust, and focus; especially to my A-Team, Wanna, Mike, Joella, Revvell, Rick, and Tara.

A big smile to the graphics team at Natural Healing Publications. You made it all seem easy.

And finally, special thanks to Capt. Bradley Green, USMC and the fighting men and women of the American armed forces who keep this country the land of the free and home of the brave. *Semper Fi.*

TABLE OF CONTENTS

TABLE OF CONTENTS

Foreword
by Dr. Richard Schulze

A few weeks ago I was doing something that I rarely do these days, personally helping a friend to heal themselves of a life threatening disease. So I agreed to spend an entire week with them and give them my best. Additionally my own reason for doing this was that I had just returned home from 2 months in Europe and even though I take GREAT care of myself while on the road, I felt after all the airplanes and restaurant meals that I could use an intensive healing week myself.

So I set up 5 days of Liver and Gallbladder Flushes, Detox Tea, Detoxification Tonic, Hatha Yoga, a barefoot 5 mile run in the soft sand at the beach, an additional hour of conditioning exercises, SuperFood Drinks, Potassium Broth, Fresh Organic Vegetable Juices, Fresh Wheat Grass Juice, Colonic Irrigations, Intestinal Formulae #1 and #2, Echinacea Plus and SuperTonic, Body Alignment Sessions, Deep Tissue Bodywork, More SuperFood, Deep Breathing, Intensive Hot and Cold Hydrotherapy, Relaxation, Meditation, Massage and Intensive Attitude Adjustment sessions for my friend, with me. All of this and more, EVERY DAY! In other words a mid-level Incurables Program. I brought in my A-Team, the best of the best, a chef to prepare the juices, teas and flush drinks, a yoga instructor, body worker etc. I also brought in the absolute best other natural healer I know, my best friend, Dr. Rocannon MacGregor.

Dr. MacGregor and I go back about 30 years, back into the 1970's. He was the only natural doctor back then that was willing to put his own ass on the line, like me, and also to play as intensely as me, many times even more. Now 30 years later he and I are still those same men, still playing hard and loving every minute of our lives. In many ways, he reminds me of . . . . ME. In many ways, he is very different. But what we both share is the absolute commitment to live our lives to the fullest and live, laugh and love every single second of every single day.

So I asked Dr. MacGregor to clear as much of his busy schedule as he could to assist me with my friend. Wow, did we have fun. Working together like we hadn't done in years. On one of his visits he gave my friend a notebook with a lot of healing information in it. A workbook to help my friend change his diseased physical, emotional and spiritual self, to stop killing himself and to start living a healthy life.

One night as he was working on my friend I laid down on an outside futon I have by my fireplace and hydrotherapy center. I picked up this notebook that Dr. MacGregor had made for my friend and I started reading it. I skimmed over this and that and then, WOW, I got to this part in the back, gems on how to live your life, and I was blown away. I started reading it and I couldn't put it down. Next thing I knew I was in search for my little yellow highlighter, to

Foreword

accent parts that I wanted to use, borrow, steal and use to change my life even more. Look friends, when the best Natural Healer in the damn world, me, gets out his highlighter, it's time to listen up.

I also immediately thought . . . I need to share this book with you, my friends, customers, health crusaders and followers, for you to have another AWESOME healing tool in your health toolbox.

Dr. MacGregor and I have been perfecting ourselves, our work and our programs, for about 30 years now. That is about 60 years of clinical practice between us. We laugh because we can't even remember who said what anymore, and whose idea it was in the first place, and WE DON'T CARE! After all these years we are very different, but also a bit of a synthesis of each other. One thing for sure. He is the ONLY other Natural Healer I know that has got the same understanding about health and healing as I do, and knows what it takes to live it, and knows what it takes to GET WELL!

Like my recent book, Common Sense Health and Healing, Dr. MacGregor's book is a book that should live with you. As soon as it is printed I plan on having a dozen copies in every room of my house, my car and even my motorcycle. And a hundred more to give to friends. Why, because just like you, I too am bombarded every day with all the negative vomit in this world. And since I am committed to great health and a great life, and I need all the help I can get, all the quotes, all the positive affirmations, all the mantras, all the healing tools, and so do you.

DO NOT read this book and then drop it. READ IT and READ IT and READ IT AGAIN. The healing jewels of wisdom in this book come from 30 years of helping others heal themselves, and 30 years of self involvement and commitment to living an incredibly healthy, loving and happy life.

I love myself, because I have surrounded myself with the finest people committed to living functional, healthy, happy, loving and fun lives. And I love myself because I have made Dr. MacGregor my friend for more than half my life. I love this man.

Please, Eat it up, and Enjoy, Grow, Laugh, Cry, Love and Heal Yourself with us.

Dr. Richard Schulze

Preface
by Marga Madhuri, Ph.D.

I can't believe it's been fifteen years, but I vividly remember that night I was going to my first yoga class with my roommate. I drove down to pick her up from work, and my car died in her parking lot. She called the teacher, who told her to put me on the back of her motorcycle and come on up. When I met Dr. Rocannon MacGregor, I felt an instant connection. Dr. MacGregor has the light, vitality, and radiance that you'd expect from a natural healer. His eyes sparkle, he speaks with a rich, vibratory voice, he moves with grace and elegance. I mean, this man is JUICY!

After class, he called me and told me he could work with me. "Great!" I said. Right out of college and fresh off the boat from Michigan, I didn't know anything about the natural healing world. But I scheduled an appointment. I don't know how I knew, but I knew he was Right. I asked my roommate what he did. She said, "Natural Healing." That didn't help me understand any better, but after my first session with Dr. MacGregor, I discovered what it meant to breathe deeply, to feel and heal old emotional charges that were locked in my body, to know myself in ways I'd never known before. More importantly, in that one session I felt that he knew and understood me better than any other person I'd ever met (including myself!)

A decade and a half later I am amazed at how much I have gotten out of working with Dr. MacGregor. My life has improved in every way—physically, mentally, emotionally and spiritually. I have healed an eight-year long bout with bulimia. I have learned to love and appreciate my body instead of neurotically despising every womanly curve, and achieved my perfect, natural body weight without counting calories or stepping on a scale. Ever. I have enhanced my communication skills, which have made me a better university professor. I have learned to accept who I am and express that to others. I have learned that first I must take good care of myself, and then I have something to share.

I have learned that health is MORE than just the absence of disease. In Dr. MacGregor's self-mastery classes, personal sessions and weekend-intensive trainings, I have learned how to live the principles of natural healing. Throughout the years, Dr. MacGregor has introduced me to a whole new world of how to live healthy in an unhealthy world. I have learned that being healthy is MUCH broader and more encompassing than I had ever imagined. Health is what you eat, what you read, how you move, how you relate, who you spend time with and how you spend your time.

Although Dr. MacGregor created this book for new clients, I find that I read and reread it over and over. The information he shares with us is vital and basic, no matter how many years we have been involved with natural healing.

Preface

In an unhealthy world, where we are pressured to skip our morning movement or get a quick (and unhealthy) bite to eat at the corner dive, we need constant reminders and refreshers to keep us on the path of wellness. Self-care is not convenient. Getting up early and going out in the cold and dark for your morning walk, packing enough food for the day—including an herbal tea for the department meeting where everyone else is drinking coffee—shopping at health food stores and farmer's markets, these take time and planning. Even after fifteen years I have to renew my personal commitment every single day. Yet, because I do these things, I am rewarded with vibrant health, enthusiasm for my work and life, and most importantly, an increasing ability to experience happiness and joy.

When you read this book, don't just let the words wash over you. Let them sink into your bones. Let them become a part of your being. Do the things Dr. MacGregor says. Consistently and Persistently. Living healthy in an unhealthy world is a Way of life.

Dig in and get the job done.

Marga Madhuri, Ph.D.

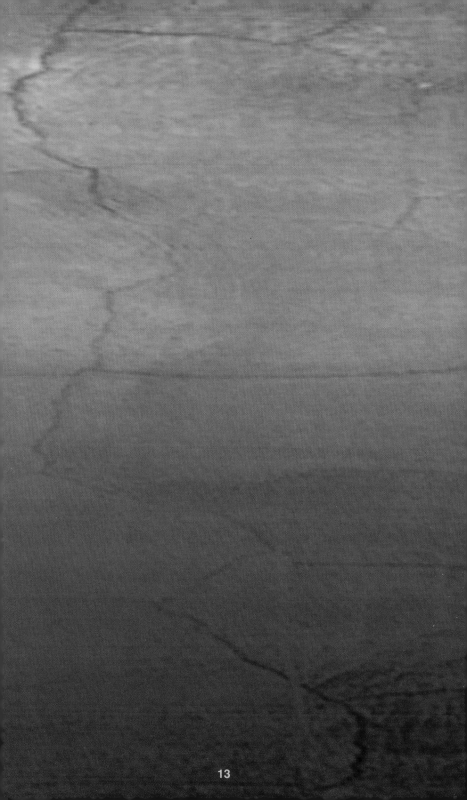

Introduction
by Dr. Rocannon MacGregor

As you study *Living Healthy In An Unhealthy World,* you should keep in mind that it began its life as a workbook for the people who came for individual sessions with me at Sanctuary (my clinic). As such, it is a collection of foundational principles, not a how-to book. Each section gives you a tongue-tip taste of what goes into making a healthy lifestyle.

How to use this book: I suggest you read it the first thing in the morning and the last thing at night for seven days. During the second week I suggest you read it at least once a day. By the third week you can flip through and re-read the sections that catch your interest. Or perhaps just go through and look at the pictures. Each one offers a reflection of healthy living and the celebration of life. Look for the story in each photo. What does it tell you?

You, of course, will determine your own way to use this book. The more you read it and explore the possibilities, the better for you. Don't hide this book. Get extra copies and share them with your friends and family. Talk about it and put it into practice. Read it on your lunch break. Read it before you go to apply for a new job. Read it while you stand in line at the store. Use it to revitalize yourself.

Living a healthy, loving, rich life requires dedication and commitment. It requires trust and courage. Reading this book will provide you with a chance to recharge and review the basic principles of healthy living, on a daily basis. Feel free to apply these life enhancing skills and principles to make your life a paradise. I still read this book even though I wrote it.

And just who am I? Well, if you like the usual details you can read the biography in the back of the book. But here is what I would like to share with you. My most important qualifications to write this book are my own daily devotion to and personal practice of Living Healthy. My daily devotion and personal practice are what make me who I am. My daily practice of Living Healthy, Living Consciously, Living Joyfully is my true qualification. By consistently and persistently applying the principles of Conscious Living, I create my life anew each day. I create my health, my wealth, and my bliss. With these skills I have transformed my life and created paradise for myself. So can you.

Applying the understanding and principles I discuss in this book, I have healed myself of recurring malaria and dysentery. I have healed myself from two motorcycle wrecks. I have not needed a medical doctor or taken any prescription or over-the-counter drug since 1969. I haven't been vaccinated or had flu shots. All my brothers-in-arms are long dead. Yet I am robust and hearty. I live this way 24/7/365. These are what I consider "real" qualifications.

My life and the lives of my clients and students have proven over and over again that these principles and skills work in the "real" world.

Natural Healing is of the people, by the people, for the people. Make it so!

Dr. Rocannon MacGregor
at Sanctuary, 2004

Get Outside Every Day

Get outside every day, first thing in the morning if at all possible. Greet the rising sun with your own radiant smile. Afternoon or evening can work too. Move across the earth with your own two feet. Hike a mountain, go for a run, go for a walk, move your body; sweat, swing your arms,

put effort into it, enjoy it. Get up to greet the dawn with your sweat and increased breathing. Get out for a second walk or hike at lunch, or in the late afternoon or evening. Learn what the weather is by being out in it, not by reading the newspaper. Whenever you get the chance to be outside in extreme weather, go for it. Go for a walk in the rain, the snow, the heat of the day, at midnight. Give your body some purposeful challenges to awaken and tone your immune system. Awaken your healer within. Most important of all, ENJOY YOURSELF in the process. This is supposed to be fun. Give yourself an attitude adjustment whenever necessary. Celebrate moving. Fun is fundamental. Remember it. ● ● ●

Move Your Body Every Day

Practice chi kung or hatha yoga, or do some simple stretching moves. Take stretching breaks several times during the day. Take time to extend and expand your body. Be sure to twist and bend and roll. Breathe deeply while you are stretching. The more ways you show yourself that you are alive, the more you will feel alive, the more alive you will be. I have a movement practice that I do every day and my life continues to be enhanced as I mature and discover myself at deeper and higher levels. You can do the same, BUT you will have to adjust your lifestyle so that it is in support of your well-being. At 54 I am feeling better and stronger than I did at 30. So can you. You can achieve a strong, healthy and vital body no matter where you are starting from today... BUT consistent, persistent, focused, effective action is required. It's up to you. • • •

Drink Up!

Be sure you drink enough water to support your physiological functioning. Pure water is essential to well-being. About 80% of my students and clients are dehydrated when they come to see me for the first time. Worse than that... they don't realize it. Dehydration creates all manner of symptoms that are frequently misdiagnosed. When I get people drinking enough water for a few weeks, many of their

symptoms begin to disappear. Drink at least one to two quarts of filtered or distilled water every day. Don't drink tap water. Get a water filter (distiller, reverse osmosis, or charcoal). I like to begin my day with a tall glass of water with a little fresh-squeezed, organic lemon or lime juice in it. I have had people tell me they don't like water. I don't care whether you like it or not. Just drink it. As you get healthier you will begin to like the taste of water. So get juicy. Drink up! ● ● ●

Let the Outside In

Open your windows and doors (literally and figuratively). Leave your windows open when you sleep. Sleep naked and use natural fiber sheets and blankets. Use cotton or wool blankets. Cotton-covered down comforters are good too. You want your whole body to be able to breathe while you sleep. Your skin acts as a third kidney and lung. Let your skin breathe. Stay in touch with your world; don't become isolated behind your walls and central air conditioning and heating. Experiment with spending a day at home with your clothes off. Experience what you are feeling and notice what you are thinking. Discover yourself. This life should be an adventure. It is filled with surprises. Enjoy them. • • •

Laughing and Smiling

Laughing and smiling are two of the most beneficial healing experiences on the planet. To have the capacity to experience the humor in a challenging situation, to be able to laugh at your own failures, to smile warmly at a stranger, friend or lover, to feel the glow of playfulness in the workplace, these are all part of a Conscious Lifestyle. As humans we are the only species on the planet that can laugh. I laugh every day. I smile simply to be smiling. It is one of the actions that brings more bliss and ecstasy into my life. And it's free! I am not talking here about laughing or smiling when you watch an entertaining movie, or hear a joke. I am talking about seeing, and being amused by, the frequent surprises, jolts, spectacles and wonders that life reveals to us multiple times, every single day. Let your laughter begin to erupt from deep inside your being. Let your laughter flow through every cell of your body. Many times a day do a smiling meditation. Smile into every part of your body, all your organs, your joints, your muscles, your cells. Just practice smiling for the sake of smiling. Notice how your attitude changes. ● ● ●

Wear Natural Fiber Clothes

Stay away from synthetic material, especially directly next to your skin. There are plenty of all-cotton clothes on the market these days. You can also wear wool, linen, rayon or a combination of any of these. If you must wear a mixed blend of synthetic and natural, try to keep it at least 50/50. Remember: You want to let your skin breathe. **Especially for women:** All-natural panties and bras. Your breasts and genitals need to breathe too. If you must wear a bra, take your bra off when you get home from work and let your chest, shoulders and breasts have a break. No tight restrictive bras ever. ● ● ●

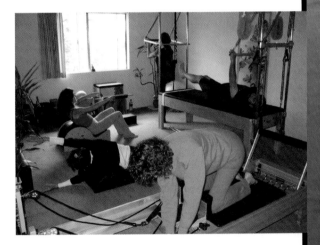

Practice Conscious Cleansing

Be aware and thorough when you bathe your body (and in everything else you do in your life). If you are going to soak in the bath, be sure to shower first, then soak, then follow with a cold shower. **Always end your bathing with a cold shower.** Use **skin brushing** (dry and wet) every time you bathe. In the shower you can use the natural fiber cloths to give your skin a good scrub and bring about a healthy glow. Soaps are not necessary, but they are sometimes refreshing.

Be sure that the ones you use are free of the usual poisons found in soaps that dry out your skin. Use a natural salt rock for under your arms. If your regular body scent is not fresh, it means you should clean up your food program, not spray on a deodorant. ● ● ●

Eat with Awareness

Eat with awareness. In other words, when you are eating a meal, be with the experience of taking in nourishment for your whole being. Smell, taste, and touch. Be fully engaged in the process. STOP when you are in the beginning of the satisfaction zone. If you notice that you are always finishing all the food in front of you, it is likely you are eating habitually, rather than with *Awareness*. When you are attentive and focused on chewing and savoring your foods, you will be aware of the moment when you have consumed enough food to fuel your body and feel comfortable. That is the time to STOP! If you over-eat, it will interfere with your digestion and assimilation no matter how good the food is that you are consuming. Keep your appetite strong by always under-eating a little bit. And stay away from quick-fix diet fads. You need to learn to eat natural foods with little or no processing. Don't bother with counting calories, carbs or fats. Eat fresh organic and living foods. Your body weight will normalize. ● ● ●

Make Time to Rest

Make time to rest. **Even a short rest or siesta can be very revitalizing.** I take 10-minute rest breaks several times during the day. Try just closing your eyes and breathing a little deeper for 5 minutes. Or get up and stretch first for a few minutes; then sit with your eyes closed, breathing deeply for a few more minutes. You'll be surprised at how refreshed you will feel. A good 10-minute rest often gives me enough energy for several more hours of productive work (or play).

Put the book down, close your eyes, and breathe for 10 minutes. **RIGHT NOW!**

• • •

Stop Poisoning Yourself!

This means no soda, no diet colas, nothing with caffeine, nothing carbonated (including sparkling water), nothing with any kind of processed sugar in it, no alcohol, no nicotine, no gum, no drugs of any kind (prescription, across-the-counter, pleasure), no flesh of any animal (vegetarians DO NOT EAT chickens and fish). I see plenty of people who call themselves Vegans who are still consuming all manner of toxic substances. Stop poisoning yourself and you will notice the difference. **Consume only that which enhances your life and well-being.**

If you really want to cut down on the subtle poisons that have a **BIG IMPACT** on your well-being, here's something else for your consideration. **Caution:** I'm really going to get tough with you now. **I'm going to hit you where it hurts, BIG TIME!** Stop watching TV, listening to the radio, and reading the newspaper. There is more mind-rotting programming in these three activities than almost any other thing that people do on a regular basis. Stop poisoning your mind and emotions with all this negative information (accurate and/or inaccurate). I have not watched TV, listened to the radio, or read a newspaper in over 30 years now. I haven't missed anything that I've needed to know. My life works wonderfully. I am happy, successful and healthy. You can be too. Stop consuming all poisons, including mental and spiritual ones! It will take some of you a long while to stop consuming all of these poisons. Do what you can do right now! Do more every day. Cleanse your body, mind and emotions. **Do it now!** ● ● ●

Actualize Your Life

As you begin to live more consciously you will free more energy for your creative use. Be sure that you channel this valuable energy into actualizing (making real through action) what you want more of in your life. Be Creative. Let your vision expand to develop a personal world where all the greatest good can easily and constantly flow in and be received. So often I have worked with people who had all manner of good things happening in and around them... but they failed to recognize these good things, they neglected to appreciate them, they disregarded or discarded the good. As

you actualize your life, be sure you are not only receiving the good that comes your way, but also appreciating it. Do what makes your bodymindspirit thrive. Make your inner-most visions real. Live life totally! • • •

You are Responsible for Your Life

You are personally accountable. When I say you are responsible I mean... "response able". That is, you are able to respond in such a way that you can make your life a continuous living miracle or a perpetual hell. It's up to you. You do not live in a vacuum. There are definite reactions to your actions. Learn how to create the life that you want. Enjoy developing your *response-abilities.* Getting and staying well requires your devotion to your self. Your entire life will transform as you apply more and more of your response-abilities and thus get healthier, stronger and more vital. It can't happen without your full participation. You are personally response-able for creating your own Good Life! What are you waiting for? Create your paradise right now! • • •

Focus on the Good

Feed and nourish the good with every action. If you aren't doing something good for yourself, why the hell are you doing it? **Whatever you direct your focus toward is what you will get more of in your life.** This is your life, and you make the difference in your life by the way you think, feel and act. Learning how to stay focused on the good, on creating and getting what you want, is the **Right Way** to live. I like to tell my students this: **"I focus so much on all the good in my life that I simply don't have any room for the bad."** In Asia it is said this way: "Nurture the good, to eliminate what is bad." Make this understanding a part of your daily practice; focus on the good, feed the good, and nourish the good. As my Grandma Nellie used to say, **"It's a great life kid, if you don't weaken."** Well, friends, I'm strong, and it is a great life. I make it so! So can you. Just do it! ● ● ●

Use Everything to Support Your Aliveness

Use everything to support your aliveness, including your weaknesses. None of you are perfect, but you can enjoy the process of perfecting and refining. To accomplish this outcome it requires that you learn to use everything that you experience in your life, to create the Good Life. You can learn to use your imperfections and obstacles as the fuel for new discoveries, personal evolution, and individual transformation. Look for opportunities. Be courageous and dare to live boldly, authentically, uniquely. ● ● ●

Be Consistently Persistent

Be consistently persistent in supporting yourself on 'The Way'. Practice the various aspects of Radiant Aliveness daily (natural foods, conscious movement, deep breathing, meditation, hydrotherapy, herbs, debriefing). What you do every day has a major impact on your life. What you do every day is your religion. Even doing little "baby steps" of Radiant Aliveness will bring about significant changes in your life. Let every day be an opportunity to create a wonder-filled life. One that you can celebrate and enjoy. My most successful clients and students consistently and persistently follow the guidelines of Natural Healing and Conscious Living. Why don't you join us? Yes, there will be times when you lose a little ground. But overall you should be experiencing life as an ongoing series of delightful opportunities and meaningful challenges. Consistently persist in living well. Don't allow yourself to be distracted by all the nay-sayers. ● ● ●

Don't Try to Teach Pigs to Sing

Don't try to teach pigs to sing, it irritates the pigs, and wastes your time. As you go about creating your conscious lifestyle... doing all this good work for yourself... I want to caution you about wasting your energy on people who ridicule, criticize or otherwise undermine your good work of building a better life for yourself. And remember: this kind of negative feed-back can, and frequently does, come from close friends, and even family members. Don't argue with people about what you are doing. Don't try and get them to do it. Don't expect them to understand and/or approve of what you are doing. Don't expect everyone you know to suddenly decide to create a better life for themselves. It isn't going to happen. I frequently have one member of a family who will develop a wonderfully satisfying life while the rest of the family continues to stumble along in their somnambulistic trance of never-lived dreams, vague hopes, and failed projects. Just focus on living your own life with integrity and bliss. • • •

Leave Others to Their Otherness

"Leave others to their otherness," is one of my favorite sayings. I like to add, "and take care of yourself first. Then you have something worth sharing." Don't waste your time trying to save others. If you will focus on taking care of yourself and doing whatever it takes to achieve your outcomes, you will find that those people around you who truly want to make a difference in their lives will begin to model your good behavior and actions. There was a woman once who took a class in body reflexology from one of my students. She became extremely interested in the class and kept pestering my student about where she had gotten her training and guidance. When she eventually found out how to contact me she immediately scheduled a session and began her own transformation. She eliminated much of her emotional baggage, freed herself from an unsatisfactory marriage, became a better teacher, developed better communication skills, enhanced her relationship skills, became a vegan, practiced yoga and chi kung and eventually went on to make her own personalized version of the "good life." In the process she had to "Leave others to their otherness, and take care of herself." Do the same and you too will have splendid results. Ignore this caution and you will end up draining your life energy away down the black bottomless abyss of people who are too afraid to risk transforming their lives. ● ● ●

Break Free!

Break free from all forms of prior conditioning, coding and programming. Learn to think and act in your favor. You can learn new functional ways of acting and efficient styles of behavior by paying attention to everything I teach you, AND then ABSORBING, INTEGRATING, and APPLYING what you have learned, throughout your life. Be attentive to which actions and behaviors actually bring you more of what you want. DO WHAT WORKS. Remember that it takes time to absorb, integrate and apply. Don't expect transformation to happen overnight, but you can expect to experience significant results fairly early in your process of conscious living... IF you do what works, consistently and persistently. Even better than that, you can expect to continue getting enhanced responses as you refine your conscious life skills. • • •

Keep it Simple!

Complex plans tend to breakdown quickly into tacky swamps of shattered fantasies and they consume excessive amounts of life energy. Do this Great Work one step at a time. This basic understanding is so SIMPLE that most people forget it. Take Baby Steps! I like simple plans that can be done NOW! Most people get so occupied with developing complex plans requiring large amounts of resources that they seldom take any effective or efficient action. Don't be one of them. Keep it simple and take baby steps. You'll go farther, and be much more likely to maintain your new Ways of Life. Keep it simple! • • •

Consume only that which nourishes and enlivens you. Eating well is actually quite simple once you break the addictions you have developed to all kinds of junk food (physical, emotional, mental, spiritual). All of us have been taught inaccurate, disastrous, disease-producing habits. Most people are not living a lifestyle; they are living a deathstyle. Consume only that which is filled with life. Vegetarian

actually comes from a Latin word that means, "filled with life." So what does this suggest? Certainly it suggests that you eat vegetables, fruits, grains, seeds, nuts and all manner of sprouted foods. These are true foods and they are filled with life. Eat at least 60% raw. I have trained world-class athletes on this kind of food program, including bodybuilders. But it also means to consume thoughts, ideas and emotions that are filled with life. It means to be alert to the kind of people you relate with and how you conduct yourself in your relating with others. **It means to be focused on consuming only those things that nourish and enliven you in every way.** ● ● ●

Open Your Elimination Channels

Open your elimination channels: thoughts, emotions, breath, skin, bowel and bladder. Get these channels open and keep them open. This is an essential principle to all Natural Healing and Conscious Living programs. Anybody who says you can be healthy or fully conscious with a clogged elimination system is, quite simply, lying. Don't kid yourself. You can't be healthy and full of morbid matter. That's not how life works. **You can't be living a healthy lifestyle and still be stuffed with toxic foods, thoughts, emotions and relationships. Get your elimination channels open, NOW!** • • •

Start Off Slow and Then Slow Down

Allow yourself the time and space to create your new life. One of the most frequent mistakes that I see new clients and students make is trying to rush their healing and self-discovery. I understand their enthusiasm, but trying to "push the river" is never going to work. In order for you to transform your life–and transformation is what you want, not just change–it will take time and space. Change is cheap. I have had clients who made a few changes and thought that was all it took to live a healthy life. WRONG! Transformation is required. Establishing new roots, developing new methods of thinking, fresh ways of acting, and continuing the process for the rest of your life. The ground of Being must be cleared. New foundations must be laid. A super-structure must be designed and erected. This all takes time and space. You must also allow for blunders, mistakes, confusion, weakness, occasional folly, and even some basic dumbness. Remember that you are not perfect. You are perfecting. Focus on polishing the facets of your being that are the most essential to your well-being. Take your time. You will be learning many new skills. Each one takes time and space to absorb, integrate and apply. A long-distance running club that I once trained with had this motto, "Start off slow and then slow down." It's good advice. Remember that you have the rest of your life to live consciously. There is no rush. Take your time, but keep moving forward! • • •

There are No Quick Fixes

When you hear about something that is too good to be true, it probably is too good to be true (except me). There are no short cuts to a good life, wealth, health, or enlightenment. You have to pay your dues and you can only *Make The Path By Walking It.* You can only do it one step at a time and you must continue doing it (remember consistent persistence). "The Way" is revealed to those who dare to take the steps. How about you, do you dare? It is risky to be Radiantly alive... but oh baby... so much fun! • • •

"Those who dare, WIN!"

Fun is Fundamental.
Seriousness is Deadly

Be sincere, of course, but Not serious. If you are going to Live Consciously and/or heal yourself, it needs to be fun. Fun is fundamental. Look at all the new things to learn and to do as fun, a joy, a delight. Don't get serious and grim about all the new skills and understanding that you are learning. Getting serious and grim is what got you sick, lazy and crazy in the first place. Stop it now! **Approach this Great Work from a perspective of playfulness.** Certainly you want to be sincere, but be playfully sincere. A sense of playfulness will immediately shift your focus and attitude. **Be happy** with yourself that you are beginning a new life. **Be pleased** with yourself that you have devoted yourself to living differently. **Take delight** in all the new actions, behaviors, ideas, feelings and sensations you are experiencing. Of course you will feel overwhelmed sometimes. This is natural. Be playful about it. Welcome the sensations of being overwhelmed with the GOOD. I have said for years, **"If you aren't feeling overwhelmed with the good, you aren't living right yet!"** To be well and live consciously you will need to learn to experience life, and all that it presents, within a different context. **Fun is Fundamental. Celebrate LIFE–whatsoever it brings! Be playful with life.** ● ● ●

People Tend to Do What People Tend to Do

Most people tend to live habitually. This includes you and everyone you know. Once you find out what a person or an organization tends to do, you will seldom be surprised. To heal yourself, to actualize yourself, you will need to investigate people and yourself on a regular basis. Some folks may tend to do well at their work and yet treat their families poorly. Others may tend to act well in front of a crowd but may tend to freeze up when faced with one-to-one relating. Stay awake and observant. What tendencies do you notice in yourself, your friends, and your colleagues? Note what is happening around and within you. Be attentive to whatever is. I debrief myself daily, sometimes several times a day. It helps me to stay focused and glowing. If you want to be different, you will have to create a new tendency. To create a new tendency you will have to practice it every single day for an extended period of time. The most difficult part of self-healing is creating the tendency to do what is good for your wellness. As you create more and more tendencies that support healing and consciousness, you will be able to maintain and expand your areas of Radiant Aliveness. Change your tendencies and you will change your life. ● ● ●

You must understand your communication partners. This is essential. Deepening the level at which you relate is vital. You certainly can't communicate effectively or efficiently if you don't understand who you are communicating with and how that person, or those people, think, perceive, and act. *What mental/emotional filters do you look through???* How about your communication partners? Remember that you must establish an interface with people, not get in their face *(interface, not in-their-face).* Intimacy is built through in-depth mutually shared discoveries and experiences, made over a period of years. *Intimacy takes time.* What most people don't understand is that intimacy is actually *"Into-Me-See."* You have to allow others to see into you and they must allow you to see into them. At that point real communication is possible. Otherwise you will always be relating superficially. Becoming comfortable with into-

me-see may take a while to develop, but it is well worth the effort. Begin the process now and reap the benefits.

• • •

More Clear Communication

Be attentive to what is behind what is said and done. Flowery language often hides deceit and cunning. Find out what motivates you and the people with whom you relate. Are they responsive or reactive? Do they have integrity? Be attentive to how you, and the people you relate with, handle success and failure. Notice what you and your associates do when you are fresh and feeling capable. Observe what happens when you, or those around you, feel tired or depressed. You want to know how you, and those around you, tend to act in differing situations. Practice becoming more aware, awake and alert. You'll be happier for it.

Notice how you and your communication partners handle the small details of living. Self-empowered people tend to take care of the small details with the same care that they would apply to seemingly more important things. Remember that there are no 'big deals', there are only lots of 'little deals' that make up what appear to be the 'big deals'. The more effectively and efficiently organized you are, the more spontaneous you can be. Taking care of the small details is an important part of good organization. Organize for full Radiant Aliveness. This is self-love. • • •

Good Deals/Bad Deals

Speaking about "deals", let me share this story with you. Many years ago I had a client who had been a drug-addict, a pimp and a murderer. He had spent many, many years in prison. By the time I met him he had radically transformed his life. Here is one insight he shared with me: "A bad deal is a bad deal. You can't make a bad deal, a good deal. The only thing you can do with a bad deal is get out of it." I frequently see my clients trying to make a bad deal a good deal. I have NEVER seen it work. But I have seen many clients wasting precious time and resources trying to make "bad deals" work. Another client shared this with me: "Don't waste your time trying to get a rock to float." So wake-up! Rocks don't float and bad deals don't become good deals. Stop doing what doesn't work and start doing what does work. Start right now. • • •

Integrity

Listen to what you and the people around you say. Watch for what is actually done. Are the words and actions congruent? If words, behaviors and actions match, you have integrity. If words, behaviors and actions do not match, you have incongruency, i.e. lack of integrity. In plain language, it means that talk is cheap. What is actually done? That's the key. Few people today have much integrity when it comes to self-care. I have people who are trying to get well while living in toxic relationships, eating junk food, refusing

to exercise, and maintaining a miserable attitude toward life. Guess what??? They don't get well. But how about the folks who are ready to live within their integrity, to face reality and do whatever it takes to transform their lives? They consistently get better. Build your integrity. • • •

Sentence Stem Completions

Sentence stem completions are a great way to get in touch with internal information quickly and efficiently. I frequently begin my day by finishing this sentence stem with at least ten different endings: "I appreciate ..." For example: I appreciate how often I speak my mind and stand my ground. I appreciate how I have sustained my conscious lifestyle for the past 30 years. I appreciate the way I organize my daily life for maximum ecstasy and bliss. I appreciate how I have created my work to be a joyous experience every day. Then I might do this sentence stem: "Today I intend..." Today I intend to continue writing my book. Today I intend to write in the park. Today I intend to focus on writing from a place of total relaxation and self-acceptance. Today I intend to ignore all external distractions. I always complete the sentence stems as quickly as possible. I don't censor or delete. I give myself permission to write out whatever comes into my mind. Remember, you can/should review and evaluate what you have written later. For a more thorough explanation of sentence stems I recommend Nathaniel Branden's book, *The Six Pillars of Self-Esteem.* ● ● ●

Appreciation and Recognition

Give yourself recognition and appreciation for what you do that makes your life better. Notice the little ways in which you are transforming. When you have made a life-supportive discipline a daily part of your life, it is a real win. Celebrate it. Correct yourself appropriately when you fail yourself. Don't beat yourself up; that doesn't help at all. Notice the pattern that led up to the failure and begin to disrupt that life-negative structure. Celebrate your triumphs and learn from your defeats. Give yourself appreciation and recognition daily.   • • •

"You can't get what you want doing what you don't want to do."
Dr. Rocannon MacGregor

Stay current with what is essential to your life. What is important to you? What do you have to do in order to maintain it in your life? You need to be alert, aware, awake, within yourself and with those you interact with on a regular basis. It is important to know the little picture and the big picture as well. **Keep your fingers on the pulse of life. Never assume anything.** Remember that the first three letters of assume spell ASS. Don't be one. Stay current. Respond to reality in a creative way. How can you stay current? Learn to breathe into your sensations. Learn to think "outside of the box." Practice living free of the old programs that have driven you to Hell every single time. Become familiar and comfortable with the happiness, joy, ecstasy and bliss that you create through conscious living. Here's a **concrete example** of what I am talking about. Last

year one of my clients accepted a position as a professor at a nearby university. During her first year she was deeply involved in adjusting to her new position. She quickly became well respected by her fellow professors and admired and appreciated by her students. However, by the beginning of the second year she realized that her life outside the university was suffering. She also recognized that her loving relationship, her daily health practices, her self-discovery and creative expression were the very things which assisted her in being a good professor. So what did she do? Well, first of all she talked with her companion, debriefed, discussed, and explored the various possible solutions. Then she gradually began to adjust her life so that there was time enough for every good thing. In a matter of only a few months she was not only doing splendidly at the university, she had also re-connected with all the good personal practices that keep her healthy, aware, alert, and conscious. By noticing when little aspects of her life were first beginning to suffer, she was able to turn the situation around with relative ease. So can you... IF you stay current with what is essential in your life. • • •

Get Right...
Take Action

When I was a little boy, Fess Parker–playing Davy Crockett–used to sing a song. The only line I can remember is, "Be sure you're right, and then go ahead." I have acted on those words for almost 50 years. Of course I can never "know for sure" that I am right. But if I am willing to stay aware, awake, alert–I can make corrections as I "go ahead." Be as aware as possible and then take action. You must take action if you are to increase your wellness, enhance your self-esteem, and create a paradise here on earth for yourself. What others do is up to them. You are responsible for what you do. Be bold. Live large!   • • •

"When the door opens, walk through it."
Dr. Rocannon MacGregor

Ask Questions

Ask questions and follow the advice of those who know 'the Way'. Self-empowered people (like myself) lead from the front. I walk and talk my Path, and I do it every single day. I live with a Radiant Aliveness 24/7/365. I am always conducting advanced experiments and explorations for my personal evolution and transformation. My life is an ongoing process. You can model these behaviors and increase the speed of your growth. When you conduct your own experiments, bring your results to your sessions with your healer, mentor, therapist or teacher for review and debriefing. I work together "with" my clients and students. They know that they are not alone. They know that they have a life mentor on their side. I have been doing this work for 30 years. I'm still learning. I'm still fascinated. I'm ready to assist them in living their lives consciously. The intelligent ones take advantage of the time they have with me. They make the most of it. They remember that they are paying me to assist them. I say to them, "Let's work together in harmony—gung ho." The ones who benefit the most are the ones who are honest, dedicated, adventurous, trusting, consistent, persistent, playful, and courageous.

• • •

Mutual Benefit

Relating with everyone should be mutually beneficial. If it isn't, you should get the hell out of it. Mutually beneficial relationships are practical, efficient and sustainable. I always work to make every interaction one of mutual benefit. With mutual benefit I am not living for anyone else and they are not living for me. Each one of us is living with an awareness of our own personal benefit. You can't have mutual benefit without first knowing what benefits you personally. When I work with my clients and students it is for mutual benefit. With mutual benefit everyone wins. There are no losers. It makes for a peaceful existence. If it isn't mutually beneficial... why are we relating? Of course there are times when I find myself in a win-lose situation. In that case I prefer to win. But those times are rare and they become even more rare as I continue to increase my skills in relating consciously. What fun! Create mutual benefit whenever possible. Remember: To have mutual benefit, you must know what is beneficial to you, first. ● ● ●

Honesty

Being honest with yourself about where you are and what you are willing and capable of doing is an essential ingredient for Radiant Aliveness. You can't get from Dallas, Texas to Los Angeles, California by pretending your are in Anchorage, Alaska. You must admit to yourself and your healer where you are starting from, what resources you have to begin with, and any other important information that has pertinence to the success of your healing process. Honesty provides a foundation for transformation. There are "lies of commission," e.g. I ask if you have been doing the self-healing program I developed with you. You answer affirmatively, even though you know that you have been "cheating" on the program. There are also "lies of omission," e.g. I ask if you have been having any drinks with caffeine in them. You answer negatively, even though you know you have been eating chocolate that has caffeine in it. Lies of commission and omission slow down your process of self-healing and definitely undermine any attempt to develop a conscious lifestyle. Without honesty in your life, you will have a "bad" reputation with yourself. This, in turn, will effect how you relate with your mentor, teacher or therapist. Life is much easier and certainly more enjoyable when you tell the truth. Do yourself a favor; be honest. ● ● ●

Just Celebrate!

Life is meant to celebrated, not suffered through. This is a foundational principle of living life consciously. Right here, right now is paradise. If you aren't living in paradise, then you aren't accepting your personal responsibility for creating it. Whatsoever life brings, you must learn to celebrate. Face life with an attitude of pleasure and excitement. When the wonders, surprises, shocks, and times of overwhelm sweep in... just breathe into the moment and handle it. It is a natural part of life to be faced with challenges. Sometimes you are going to lose. But knowing how to celebrate whatsoever life brings will allow you to win from your losses. Suffering is for drama/trauma kings and queens. Celebrating life every moment is for those of us who choose to live blissfully.

• • •

Upper Limits

Raise your Upper Limits of Joy, Bliss and Ecstasy. It is essential that you recognize that there is a very good chance that you will sabotage your own growth, healing and well-being. I know it sounds crazy that anyone would sabotage his or her own good, but it is true. It is a well-researched fact that many people have happiness anxiety and success anxiety. Although it may sound crazy, it happens frequently. The way it usually begins is that you will begin to feel anxious as your life gets better and better. Getting healthier, developing more wellness, increasing your consciousness is unfamiliar; it isn't "normal." As you begin to approach what has been your previous Highest Good, your anxiety increases. You begin to feel uncomfortable; it doesn't feel like "you." Generally speaking, when people begin to experience anxiety they do something to reduce the anxiety. At this point, if you are not careful, you will begin to do something to lower your good to more familiar, and thus tolerable, levels. That is, UNLESS... you break through your previous Upper Limits and establish a new and higher level. If you do break on through and raise your Upper Limits, you will have created more functional living space. If you continue to evolve you will have to continue raising your Upper Limits again and again.

I have had to raise my Upper Limits literally hundreds of times during the past 30 years. As a matter of fact, as I continue to get better at manifesting everything I want, I also have had to get better at pushing my Upper Limits higher and higher. The few times when I have gotten careless, have proven to me how easy it is to undermine my own good... and not even notice until I found myself back in a familiar comfort zone. Yikes! Be attentive to your Upper Limits and learn to grow beyond your anxiety of happiness and success. This will push your boundaries out into unknown and uncharted spaces. These are the spaces where you can create a new and evolved self. ● ● ●

Share Your Self

Share your love, compassion, appreciation, and gratefulness every day. You might do this with a colleague at work, a person you meet in a store, a friend or a lover. It doesn't matter who it is. Share your Robust Vitality, no matter what level you are at in the moment. It doesn't have to be a big deal. Little gestures are also powerful. Spread the joy, the happiness, and the bliss. I give appreciation every day to my clients and students. I share my compassion and gratefulness regularly. By doing so I am increasing my own awareness of just how wonder-filled my life is. The more you share your love, your laughter, your strength, the more you will know you have it to share. If you don't use it, you lose it! So what are you waiting for? Share your aliveness today and every day. ● ● ●

Do Your Homework!

Read books that assist you in your self-actualization. Here are a few recommendations to get started:

The Healer Within
by Dr. Roger Jahnke

Six Pillars of Self-Esteem
by Nathaniel Branden

Philosophy of Natural Therapeutics by Dr. Henry Lindlahr

Healing with Whole Foods by Paul Pritchford

How I Found Freedom in an Unfree World by Harry Browne

The Complete Book of Chinese Health & Healing by Daniel Reid

Polarity Therapy-Vol. 1 & 2 by Dr. Randolph Stone

While I don't agree with everything in these books, there is a lot of useful information, which, if used properly, can assist you in creating your individual Healing Lifestyle. Don't waste your time with magazines and newspapers. If you are going to make the time to read, make it worthwhile and life-supportive. • • •

How Long Do I Do It?

I have people, good people, who ask me, "How long do I have to do this program, diet, exercise, breathing, etc.?" Every time I am asked, even after 29 years in practice, I am still surprised by this question. Here is my typical response: "What I am teaching here is the Way to live with full Conscious Radiant Aliveness. I suggest that you absorb, integrate and apply the principles every day for the rest of your life. Why would you consciously choose to poison yourself again, make yourself sick again, debilitate yourself again? Why would you want to go back to bad habits, habits that are self-destructive? Why would you want to create paradise and then purposefully destroy it?" ● ● ●

The Conscious Lifestyle I teach is the cure for the disease of modern people; it is a way of producing the internal medicine of life, a way of awakening the healer within. It is a Way of living Consciously, Radiantly, and Joyfully for all the days of your life. If you want to be vital, vibrant, creative and juicy, then you will apply what you learn for the rest of your long and fruitful life. Anything less is a crime against wisdom.

~Rocannon MacGregor, Founder of the Feast~

Teacher of Natural Healing & Conscious Living

October 2003

About the Author

In the late 1960's, Dr. MacGregor served three tours of duty in Viet Nam as a Marine Combat Platoon Leader. During this time he came in contact with a local native doctor. In a small remote jungle village, this healer was the man to see if you had problems of any kind–physical, emotional, mental or spiritual. He used acupuncture, herbs, hydrotherapy, moxa, cupping, body therapy,

Rocannon MacGregor, USMC
Viet Nam 1968

food, movement, breathing, counseling and meditation. He helped the local folks live, love and prosper, all of this in the midst of a war that had been going on for over 30 years. This man was Dr. MacGregor's first teacher of Natural Healing. For two years he trained with him and assisted him in his clinic, a bamboo hut on the outskirts of the village. This experience would end up changing his life, forever.

Dr. MacGregor received his honorable discharge and returned to the United States where he knew he had work to do. This is when he began his personal journey into Natural Healing. Upon arriving home he built a small lean-to in the remote forest near Wolf Creek, Arizona and lived there alone for an entire year. In Viet Nam he was exposed to some of the worst toxic chemicals known, like Agent Orange, and was infected with numerous deadly diseases like Malaria. To cleanse and balance himself after the war he did hours of hydrotherapy in the ice cold creeks and hundreds of sweat lodges, along with hours and hours of meditation.

His first formal training came directly under the great Dr. Randolph Stone, D.C., N.D., O.D., the founder of the Polarity System of Natural Healing. He then completed his advanced training at the Polarity Health Institute.

He trained additionally at the Eclectic School of Natural Healing, where he learned the principles of life energy including Western Nature Cure, Ayurvedic Medicine, and Oriental Medicine. He studied the arts of manipulation, botanicals, counseling, nutrition, movement, breath, hydrotherapy, hypnotherapy, counseling, psychotherapy, Hatha Yoga and Chi Kung. He also interned with Dr. Vivian Morris and numerous other Naturopathic and Chiropractic Physicians.

It would be difficult to find any Natural Doctor with more training and certifications than Dr. MacGregor. His studies have taken him to remote areas of the world such as Bali, India and China. To list some of his accomplishments he is certified in: Polarity Therapy, Medical Chi Kung Therapy, Functional Kinesiology, Structural Integration, Zen Shiatsu, Cranio-Sacral Therapy, Spinal Touch, Kiatsu, Myopractic,

About the Author

Neo-Reichian Therapy, Body-Centered Psychotherapy, Transpersonal Therapy, Psycho-Emotional Integration, Neuro-Linguistic Programming, and Hypnotherapy. Additionally he has trained extensively and is certified to teach in seven different styles of Internal Healing Arts and is a certified Hatha Yoga Instructor.

Dr. MacGregor has always said that all the above trainings and certifications are of minor importance compared to his 30 years of clinical experience working with his clients and students at his Sanctuary. He says that it has been in the day-to-day interaction with them that he has learned some of his most valuable lessons. It is in Sanctuary that he has had the opportunity to share, explore, discover, and develop Living Healthy in and Unhealthy World. • • •

"Adapt. Improvise. Overcome."
Dr. Rocannon MacGregor

A Final Note

from

Dr. Richard Schulze

→

A Final Note

From Dr. Richard Schulze

I published Dr. MacGregor's book as part of my continuing commitment to educate you in Natural Healing, to empower you to heal yourself and live a long, healthy life.

Congratulations for taking the time to read this book. If you follow the principles in this book and add them into your daily life, you will change. You will stop repeating the victim's mantra of *why me* and will gradually free yourself from dis-ease. Better yet, you will build a powerful, long lasting, happy and healthy life.

As you have read in this book, Dr. MacGregor is big on action. What is in this book won't heal you, but living it will. One way you can start living it right now is to begin some of his fundamental programs like increasing your nutrition and opening up your elimination channels. This is where I can help you.

I encourage you to call my company, the **American Botanical Pharmacy,** toll-free, at **1-800-HERBDOC (437-2362),** and ask for my FREE introductory package to be sent to you. I will send you an audio tape, a book, and other educational healing tools.